Life and Times of Mr. S

Life and Times of Mr. S

Vivek Narayanan

HarperCollins *Publishers* India

First published in India by
HarperCollins *Publishers* in 2012

Building 10, Tower A, 4th Floor, DLF Cyber City, Phase II,
Gurugram Haryana – 122002, India
www.harpercollins.co.in

This edition published in India in 2020 by HarperCollins *Publishers*

2 4 6 8 10 9 7 5 3 1

P-ISBN: 978-93-5357-608-0
E-ISBN: 978-93-5357-609-7

Typeset in 10.5/14 Minion Regular at
SURYA

Printed and bound at
MicroPrints India, New Delhi

to Rashmi

CONTENTS

ACKNOWLEDGEMENTS

Some of these poems have appeared, in differing versions, in th following journals:

Manchester Review: 'Short Prayer to the Economy', 'Waking i the Simultaneous Present'

Poetry Review (UK): 'In-law of S'

Blackbox Manifold: 'Nature, As Manifested in the Higher Altitudes of the Indian Subcontinent'

International Literary Quarterly: 'He Admits He Is Delirious in Thinking of How He Carried Her', 'Hiding from Rhetoric's Shadow'

Pratilipi: 'On the Necessity of Speaking of Caste'

Tehelka: 'Mr S, on First Looking into Parthasarathy's Cilappatikaram'

With + Stand: 'Mr S's Data', 'Short Prayer to Sound', 'Digression on Receipt of Nourishment, Acknowledgement of the Body's Inbuilt Guilt'

Almost Island: 'His Own Obsolescence: Six Shapes of the New', 'Poem, with Choices'

Special thanks to those friends who read and commented on this manuscript in its various drafts; and to the India Foundation for the Arts and the Ratan Tata Foundation for a grant during which time these poems were written.

WAKING IN THE SIMULTANEOUS PRESENT

Enter, in the very mist   of awakening's wrangle
a sudden but not unusual recall
                    of being alone
in the afternoon another life   a code
in the noisy determinedly disinterred burr
of the brain.
                    Does it matter if it counts
as a dream?   In that mild
afternoon he walks   happy and
in the morning of this poem   he wakes
happy, alone but as he rises
to boil the milk   switch on
the geyser   the additive effect
of more than one happiness
is somehow sadnesses:
                    afternoon already coming
to this place,
                    already going
from that one
                    his coat put away
    the ceiling fan resuscitated
  and summer, deadly summer   wrangling its brand

of bright decaying   pustulant life. Human,
alone   with his sponging self
and like the suicidal pigeons   on the ledge
        Master S himself
is not quite   cracking the code
of the succession
of instances
that is he (reality
would be
my favourite movie
a friend said, except
that it never begins).

A BRIEF EXPLANATION OF MR S'S ACCENT

The simple if mildly scandalous truth was that his
    accent changed. Close attention to its
timbre might allow a new faith in the fact of
    continuous revision; accent not an
indisputable centre but a desire, an attuning beyond
    certainty sprung in that lush early
valley of surplus identity, a valley where decision was
    unashamed and the real accent was
on how and when and whether
time became hard or supple
in the course of this unfolding.

HIS OWN OBSOLESCENCE: SIX SHAPES OF THE NEW: 1

One Day

That he might, one day, slough off this hokum of him,
merge into a purity of form.
That in this emerging the world was still remaindered in
the texture of its husk.
That, failing that, he might suddenly wake up in the midst
of the shake-up, in the face of its blinding face, just
to call himself back up for a second, say hi.
That one day in a glint he might come to understand what
it is he is hotly writing now.
That one day we may dare again to judge between aura
and monochromatic fetish, belief being a value and
not an event.
That that might be the start of something new.

O static noise meadow! O days of looking forward to Wonder Balloon!

Oh, intellectual, intellectual toy!

AREA OF MR S

And he hurt his way back into that mess,
that black unchangingness,
those trees with their khaki leaves,
old slow avenues,
those yellow painted squares,
zebra skinned pavements – how
sharp and mysterious the chequerboard
of edges when the zebra of
the curb pale itself and ghostly guided! –
and he followed his way to that old home
under the coconut tree
punctuating the dusty mess
of a square, the underclothes
of scooters parked unaware,
the old woman squatting perpetual
at the gate (once he almost spoke to her
but for the treeless triangle between them
confoundingly great) – and despite the place
its stress on stillness in the continually unfurling summer,
the noise of the evenings he mingled with idols
on their languid circular tours

or those frowning improvised thickets of bulbs,
the back he turned to that yellow
and the face it turned to him, sharp
citadels of plastic packet
and silver wrapper, heaps clarifying
to unembarrassed
elbows, startling lack
of policemen despite the police
residential quarters just there –
that secret shortcut square,
hidden idyll, its
sudden conjurings of space fried
likewise in recurring Saffola –
or zigzags of inextinguishable shops and
quickly expandable multicoloured goods,
overlaid self-spellings on the new tin
of old sign, to walk into and in walking
zippingly sense out the mess,
the jest darkening under trees
of ashen indeterminate age
and people crooked like branches back
back into an unacknowledgeable past
where too someone ambled – even Thiruvalluvar
a wide-eyed confused young man greater than
today's frozen plaster – and in leaving to forget such
that in a hardening crook
of his own spine sets
that un-notatable pause
parsing each iteration
with the lingering archaic transliteration

hammered on the plate
of a corner, an egress, a jumbled nook
spattered on wave-lashed stone –
to open that packed sandwich
with the grace of unmasking sun.

MR S, ON FIRST LOOKING INTO PARTHASARATHY'S CILAPPATIKARAM

On my street, the little peeps of car horns reign. From far above
from the balcony from where I am   admittedly political

it is very much like being squeezed in the arm. And yet my total
memory torments me oh that I might

like Kannagi
chuck my burning breast at the untrue city

in the metre of sweet-mango-fruit, sour-mango, sweet-mango,
sweet-mango-fruit –

it is late in the current century; our esteemed Master S
without yet wife
without issue yet yet
holding pen in hand with sweetly consecrated Kannagish grief
without necessarily due cause
without registry-entry, nearly though quaintly political
without kingdom to reign or release entirely at the mercy of the
elected warlords and their respective sub-warlords
without once being known to them by name

with neither rein of nor consequence to his words
sitting at the laptop without sitting
unstable as any system organic or synthetic
fraying at the edges into ether
reined in by little more than luck
resisting the daily teleportation

without need nor power to provide it
without much hope of unaccidental death
with enough mango fruit sweet to tide the monsoon through
with light touch of winter in the veins
without fear but rather a latent dread
without any semblance of practical politics and yet somehow
political
with love for the mysteriously unmysterious grey hornbill, its
archaic beak waddling ungracefully still in a tree-hole of
the refumigated garden
without an acre of land or a portion to call his own
with infinite sensory register but without much by way of names
or gradations for such data luscious in dusk
smog beautiful and deadly as a visual bell puffing up from unseen
manufacturing units particles like diamonds in this, like gems
leaping from an anklet that once she our Kannagi wore
that once and forever led to her our Kannagi being recognized
without being known
which is to say being misrecognized in the walled city where
everybody was thought to be known

which is to say tragedy always in the guise of a stranger an anklet
like some kind of fake identikit
which is to say Mr Subramaniam our friend our friend in our

own image without rein of horse-cart   without ticket
to space station
which is to say nevertheless let us not mask our bourgeois difference
which is to say not without the ability to register a certain daily
grateful quota of iota pleasure
not without the sweetness of sweet the tartness of fruit
the cheapness of pens even when one is ridiculously
picky about one's choice of pens
which is to say rich and free enough from the political to be able
to luxuriate in the political

which is to say   nevertheless   of ambiguous and shifting class
background not unlike forgive me not unlike Kannagi not
quite royalty not quite poverty
without much to complain about but without the lack of
rumination to not complain about it
which is to say without pretending to reign   either with pen or
with intergalactic ballistic missile
which is to say the sweet mango fruit of SMS sex metre but
without once the banishment of longing
which is to say how exactly does an ancient text register in the
soggy wafer of a brain scrambled by all registers   O but it
does it does

without being apolitical but nevertheless sweet as a mango and
sometimes angry indiscriminately angry   like a roadside
Kannagi ready to end the reign contra the truth of love say
Oh this is where you were going all along Mr S to his racing
pen   oh penmani   register for me at least that link to what
was perpetually being lost even then in that dreamtime
to our still troubled times

rein in the true political   bring out weak and spineless testicularly
encumbered man your truer Kannagi   your   inner kanmani
your truest courage   your missing breast   step by step
minute by minute   stand   turn back   look   look hard and
devour my dear sir   the sweet mango fruit of that vision.

SHORT PRAYER TO THE ECONOMY

prayers for fishes, tossed each to each in translucent glue
prayers for the hairier beasts, roistering in rolling tundra
if we are to conceive a world, let us conceive it – at all risk – one

prayers for the wily bicycle, knight of secular propulsion
prayers for uncoagulated human residue impossible to
    weigh in balance
and our economy that intricate grows, beyond forbearance

I've found I don't know I need I to know who can I talk to
who can I call what must I do where must I put it how can I
use it what is your number who will you call where will we go
how will we make it where will we put it who can I finger how
will they take it where is the button how can I find it how did
he get there who does he know what can it do where does it
go how do you work it what will it work take what it will work
it you do how does it where what can it do who does he know
who did he get there how did he find it how is the button
where will they take it how can I finger who will we put it
where make it how we will go where call you what who number
how how must I put where do I must what call I can who talk
to I who can to know I need I know I don't I found I feed

prayers for the musical crow, the intimate mosquito,
    whose kisses are here to say
prayers for the contract killer, the contractual signer, unspeakable
    unimpeachable bond
and our shared godless theology that hooks the day to day

prayers for all projectiles, red, yellow – somewhat bluish, spinning
    inert, riskily pulsed –
prayers for gashes of quarried stone, saunas of smelted aluminium,
    ever thinning veins of copper
from where the monstrous weather grows

Feed I found I don't I know I need I know to can who I to talk
who can I call what must I do where put I must how number who
what you call where go will we how it make where it put we will
who finger I can how it take they will where button the is how it
find he did how there get he did who know he does who do it can
what where it does how do you it work will it what take work it
will what it work you do go it does where do it can what know he
does who there get he did how it find I can how button the is
where it take they will how finger I can who it put we will where
it make we will how go we will where call you will who number
your is what use I can how put it I must where do I must what call
I can who talk I can who know to I need I know don't I found I've

prayers for the intestinal tract, whose winding road grows hidden
prayers for the rickety aeroplane, suspended in the air
the prickly fog will take us, will all of us be spared

prayers for every scrawny stick uncountable, each that I know
    by name
prayers for the murderous author, the deadened reader,
    the wakening good
and lastly that arithmetic not of our making, its obsolete fire

Sex, which after all is mechanics, ought to be straightforward.
Those who start out as prodigies are doomed to be late bloomers.

HIS OWN OBSOLESCENCE: 2

Terror of the Offering

And what about the glints of foil among the rice offerings
(shocking how the old gods look so up to date with
    their neo-classical
forms!) what about the yokel hokum that does still somehow
    address suffering,
what about the bright panoramas of fear, the coconut
    head broken, the quizzical
old sickle in the hands of the newly desperate? Ah, time itself
    is fetishized,
shaken up from within by the re-detonation of the always:
    finished.

And here in
the place of writing, the taps
always hissing.

THE ZYGOTE'S FIRST UTTERANCES

In a dim alley, the last microcosmic blue sparks of a soldering flame. Then the grey – a curtain, both metaphysical and mechanical, both a lack of colour and its own kind of heat – descends.

The rain roars unseen: imagine it in that putrid after-smell, the broad reflective puddles mingling with the road.

From within, the fatigue wisping like smoke.

I am a machine; I begin at zero. My metal speaketh a message.

I'm alive, I'm a generalist. I measure millenia.

All the equipment I have is essential, O Garbarakshambika; ether is no evidence, and yet, as a word, it too aspires to exactitude.

NATURE, AS MANIFESTED IN THE HIGHER ALTITUDES OF THE INDIAN SUBCONTINENT

Take one. 'They have a strange thing in these hills,' Mr S's companion informed him. 'They like to plant the same pear trees everywhere. Locally, these are called "Wallberries", for reasons that may or may not have to do with walls.

'We seem to lack the natural imagination of the land, sir, of nature's multifoliate spring. We think in careful relation, in ones and twos. We lace the eyes with limited saliva.'

'To grow is to suppress; to cultivate, lie,' said S.

'Indeed. Us humans, always we are simply singing our sad lieder solo, sir. How we like to make the land edible and positively peachy, no? Then what? Licking salt in earth wounds, mostly pervertedly. And complaining of bad relations! Complaining in verse, no less. Mending walls, but shruggingly so.'

'Hmmm.' Truth though it may have held, Mr S perhaps resented the reference.

They walked on. In these moderate hills spring always lurks round the next corner, ready to be sprung on the unsuspecting, ready to thrill or startle, to relate the itinerant walker to geological time. As a matter of fact, any moment now he expects Auden, still cute, still young, to jump out, naked, with a canoodling dildo in his hands.

'The lounging older world, sir, is entirely capable of constructing and destructing itself.'

And yes, *despite* that peach-bloom glaze, this still triumph. Amazing, really, that beauty had managed to survive photoshop in this way, but it had.

Take two. Chug-chugged, the little toy train, so emblematic and so utterly useless.

Snort, snort, said the truck, importing gravel from the plains.
Salt and chillies, said the man to his mound of rice.
And the pear trees lined the wall; the fruit grew fatter, fatter, the summer rained on.

Take three. Oh the hills, their cast of quirky characters, their simple phrases salting the morning talk, their work-song, their spring- and winter- song. Their peach and pear trees, their unnaturally beautiful dogs. Their insistence, almost by definition, on not progressing, as the plains do. And the immense mind-work to keep this fantasy alive, to keep the crows (for they are plentiful) and the parking garages (for they are continuous) from crowding out the frame.

Take four. Beauty of speech in the evening air. Sprung rhythm. Relations with capitalism for sure, but perhaps a little less in your face.

Take five. Spit it out, the beautiful lie!

Take six. Somehow, in answer to the question, 'Are we happy here?' the answer is usually, even in relentlessly gloomy weather: 'Yes.'

:

reason: here is your longed-for horizon,
let all eat all, let my backside face
the sky, head follow
the zagging river's course:
I shall give my throne away.

SHORT PRAYER TO SOUND

Sound has the particular quality of being visible. It is the greater god. Vision, in evening's fog, shows a man on the cycle with his newspaper bags, the threaded breeze of his hair, the holes of his eyes; yet, though riveting, vision knows nothing of his pain.

Sound does, for sound is pain, curled and garbled by the ganglia, stunned and suppressed, dim thundering from some secret window. Never regular, though it may sometimes seem so. Never present, though it may seem. Rivet of moment to moment. A sack on the face with holes to see.

Imprecise, as a world seen through cloth, ease of the friend that follows. Agony internal to the shape. The tinier holes through which a quality refines. A private lack, a riveting in some riveting act.

What does sound carry? It will not tell. It refuses to be known. So close to us, clinging, it will not tell. He wants to gather memories in its sack, as if memories in the brain's shifting imagos had actually the tangible quality of being gatherable. Alas, sound is forgetting. It has already been forgotten. It is the hole into which all knowhow disappears. A hole we can only call: *the future.*

Yet, like peas in a pod, like arguments in the agora, it follows tracks.

ON THE ADVENT OF THE ZYGOTE, SOME NOTES FROM S TO WIFE

This excitation of our inner elements: all of existence as no more
than experiment from end to end.

Our self-education in the art of each other; the grand inefficiency
of it; the shaggy, static electric that sometimes misfires
between us.

Yet, accruing by the tiniest fractions, our fluctuation has bound us,
aligned us. Moves inside you now, millimetre by millimetre.

We soar between the fundamental swaras. Their genius lies
in waiting.

Wait: mystery and mysticism are not to be mixed but

factor in our faith: it is weightless, changes nothing.

Each of the faces you find finds yours.

ON THE SUPPOSED SIMPLICITY OF THYAGARAJA

It is said an artist lives on love. Thyagaraja had no time for the king, so it is said. It is said that ardour is the father of work; the seed will not be shown in the diagram today. The motor moves as if unwilled, corkscrews through the rose

of an inner ear or the rose of pure colour in the sea of time; old-fashioned time, as if the beat before Thyagaraja's less-than-innocently delayed first note were left to its own. And in the cavern of that ardour lies the morning sea, the oldest sea, and in it the fisherman's indelicate boat with a small motor

and tiny flywheel at the back, a toy. O thought-seed, seed that wanders from wild shore to king's impeccable garden – let us pluck, in passing, that imported rose – seed that travels via buffalo dung or diesel, seeding present with pasts:

had Thyagaraja actually seen his blue-bodied god?

Ugh. For the phone's gone dead, no tone, no hum, just hiss.

For I too have longed for visions in the swim of my ardour, I too have longed to shuck the shell of this, my improvised device.

Help me, heavenly motor, celestial circuit-board, powerline incarnation, spark-producer!

'He rose to drink a glass of water
and noticed a sudden blue glow,
its source a slat below the door.'

Thyagaraja,
on the other side,
didn't sing a thing.

The net's faint white gauze vanished in rose light.

But the water spills in that light! In the heart of your voice's ardour there is an absence of ardour. Something does not shake.

The seed still threatens to sprout in Subramaniam's mouth.

And no one has left you to your own. The world – its matter-parade – is incapable of abandonment, dear. Heard that? He has drawn your seed from his very mouth, hey Thyagu.

Crackling, a second voice
Crackling, a second voice from the improvised device.

NIECE OF MR S

Lulu, did you know, this morning Mr S
        walking into a town crossed the canal
                on a rough and weedy stone bridge at least
                        500 years older than you or

me. The factories and the fields slept side by side, a man
        on a scooter blinked and waved, a woman
                in a pagoda hat dug in the soil with her fingers
                        a donkey groaned as donkeys do and

Lulu, did you know, no one remembered themselves
        or where exactly in the face of that morning wind
                they were, that fresh smell
                        in the air and probably the planet

itself had forgotten with no duties except to spin
        happy like the toy it was. Lulu, time makes no day
                the same. Lulu, even when you
                        were born a tiny beast in a wicker cradle we

knew that you came not from some bland
        baby fact but were made
                unique and unlike all the other humans
                        before. Lulu, it is still in your power

to be unlike. Lulu, we grow so big we lose
        the power to be small, then our toys
                are toys no more; Lulu, did you know, the donkey gazes
                        at the field with a wide look it cannot

complete; the human hand changes, uncommon, expensive,
        weird; then the cheap robots refuse to make
                mistakes, doing their duty blind
                        to duty. Lulu, I remember your

paintings or the cards you've made, the way shapes
        take jagged jumps in swirling scribbled fields
                of red and green and you must not lose that even
                        if you get bigger your eyes command

your hands grow deft. Lulu, it is your duty to keep
        this world from turning the same; Lulu,
                now I will draw you a key in these last lines
                        knowing it to be a kind of a toy:

a factory swaying (for we must keep
        the factories too) swaying in the morning wind
                that runs yellow speckles through
                        the brown and green field and

the skies dim slightly and the water sings as it runs through
in strokes; a white yawn of a cloud hovers, a barge
slips humming under the bridge; and you
and I are creatures walking on

the planet as it turns and turns.

MR S'S NATIVE

'Twas a time not long ago when Mr S, entirely, blissfully, comfortable in a second-class train compartment, might well have been asked, 'Sir, where is your native?'

Which is to say, short for *native place*, which is simply to ask not where you have come from, nor where you're coming from, but where you

come from. Which is to say,

for poor Mr S, a rather great difference between fairly firm and carnival jango on precipice edge.

For tell me, troublesome gods, shall nativity be allied with birth or shall it be carried to its limit in genes one direction and genes
 the other? And,

does it count if your birth was followed in seconds by a change of scenery? Are you indeed eligible at the razor edge of spoken language? Can it still be your native if you are, by virtue of indelible travels, no longer very native? Is it only Mr S in whom such questions elicit carnivals of angst, orgies of self-disapproval?

In other words, is it possible to leave a place? And if so, is it possible to return to that selfsame place? Is it possible to immaculately give birth to me-ness, me-ness as subset of us-ness, which is to say the nonstop carnival in the nanosecond of the eyeblink of a theoretical true native?

Mr S is nervous. Such questions may well drive him to the edge's edge, a place where no native shall be allowed the slightest chance of survival. Chop! Birth has been outlawed in S's secret land. And yet –

and yet, in a second life
a dream in which there is no carnival of parting,

and where carnival is no parting but instead the gauge of that second place where Mr S might be finally born as native. Stranger things have been known to happen to the non-native, after all:

once our hero was lost at a great fair, upper torso that of an adult's but legs just-birthed baby, and as he struggled to steer himself past the strong man and his stunts and the street theatre, insipid except for a man with a gash across his face, Mr S loved them all and loved that circumstances made it impossible for him to stand out

and everyone was streaming towards the edge of the grounds where one entered a place of enclosure where

rapt crowds heard speeches.

Such politically percussive speeches!

Mr Sub-sub, hog-happy, laughing, crowd-synchronized, arms raised then akimbo, cheerleader Subraman-i-am lost in the glue of talk, the first speaker, then the second,
and the third, and the second again.

This was the dream of the event and
Mr S attended both editions.

As for the real event, a knot of policewomen firmly prevented entry to the grounds and the poor lamented the lack of large outdoor screenings of the speeches given inside, at least, for their pleasure and as thank you for time out from work.

Ah well, Mr S, how about that?

The poor are the nativest, sir, and yet no place is home for them.

HIS OWN OBSOLESCENCE: 3

Things

No doubt there is the vice
of the new, some
kind of glandular
shake-up in every
restitutive fetish, some
screwed-up eros of
object hawking
its hokum yes but
nevertheless
irresistible – the arch of a
ladle reminds you of
her neck, so lickable! then
right after that an ordinary
headlamp glints, so weirdly
strokable! and you wink
back without hardly
thinking it,
damn it!

MOTHER OF MR S

Amma, the dignity with which you carry yourself
perplexes me, your setting a moral pluriverse right with
each decision each parry each darting
forestalling glance forward

Mother, the four of us exchange our energies
in the face of multitudinous atrocities you calmly refuse
to believe in evil Mama the world
and its phenomena do not

concern you but yet Mummy how I admire
and am muddled by the manner your
yoking of pride and diffidence
in single being in

appearing aloof not out of snobbery
but rather at necessary times in the wait
of something authentic festering
unsaid Ah Ma you ruined

me you stung me with your insistence
in stern face on the true and it frightening
in the kitchen that nameless afternoon
the four-cornered door opened on the back yard

and I looking out there that endless yellow grass
asking but O Mata can't I tell a lie what can
happen who can do what to me if I do
can't a lie show as well a lie as faint
as the grass is long as tiny as brief

as the bee that stung my eye that mashes
the hurt to make this yard like all the yards can't
I can't I tell one just like walking like the first day you let
me run out there and play

by myself one not wrong but only a kind of carriage
to end all lies in the paternal play of the sky for
we know well I can confidently say now
though I didn't then that the lie

in truth precedes the truth and you
stiffened and said in the certainty of
your forestalling code No no kanna no no
matter what you must never

never tell a lie and I could not forget
you saying that just as I cannot
forget my not looking at you but
rather at that open door and the vista

that called to me unending Moder how even now
I want never to be like you and even
now I want exactly to be like you
and I am exactly like you and

the sunlight leaves and not
a shadow moves and I ask of the world
its immovable stones not least
in search of an independent

incorruptible authority well which
is it must I am I like her or un-
like her but not even an echo
returns to answer nor faith
arrives to anchor yet Mamma I love

how you carry yourself like a head of state and
although the seven oceans and the four
continents still sing your desperate
praise you are calm appear unconcerned even

if you are worried for me and by extension
for all of humanity and though Aayi love
is intense and troubled in all the every
language born from it one could

argue for S's mother's son's sake that thaayi
paasam as it appears in the Tamil tongue
is most intense and troubled of all even to
the very point of murder yes but

Mamma let me underline nevertheless
I myself have no intentions whatsoever
of killing you rather it embarrasses me
to write these words that is to size

myself in order that they be written for
despite what you once said about
your own writing which remained
hidden from me those years
even as clearly it was somehow carried

and quartered into me as insuppressible inexplicable
aspiration and when I understood where it was
things do come from and where they sometimes lead
you told me how endings were such

a problem that you Maman were tempted to finish
each tale of yours by simply killing the central
character since that ease of exit does in theory exist
even as nothing can really be that easy in

there for the equivalent reason that it
is not so simple out here and in fact
utterly forestalling the apparent gap
between our worlds is that they

are not worlds at all except in a manner
of speech and perhaps the greatest
secret both unpleasant and
not is not that death is continually near

us which fine it is but rather Mom
that things which are both the particular
plastic buckets and swollen ankles and not
are unable to end and they like little dustmote

variant patterns must will persist resist persist

o let it dangle then that disinterred afternoon
let alone be the code for human
for in our oneness our crinkled codes will diverge
in the alone afternoon I enter as human

You have come to the conference late.

HIDING FROM RHETORIC'S SHADOW

(Duet with Mrs S)

If you blur, my love, it is only
because we are close. The waking west
beats time upon my skull; that night
it widens in a collective mouth. To
whom is this gift of the already built
given, to whom it unhindered go?

> *I know you are so anxious, dear,*
> *before the sprout might pierce*
> *the surface, before the dead chance*
> *to revive. But the noise it drains me too, remember,*
> *and my words, once spoken, evanesce.*
> *Must you hold me like an empty vessel?*

Forgive me, my love. Their armies somehow
entered; now they guard each cell and
membrane. And some voices are so clear
in the din: the TV's circulating bang bang,
the paper's forever grey. Day after day the spell
goes on. Everyone has their say.

Yes, everyone has their say. The air so thick
with assumed allegiance. And despite
the lawns so tidy, the skin
so bright in a mist of spring
no one is allowed to be happy.

But the speed of rhetoric at my heels!
I cannot run fast as once I did.
The gunman in his tennis shoes
leaping from right to right
somersaulting from west to west
into my vulnerable heart.

If you blur, my love, I suppose
it's because we are close.
Is there room in our house for others?
Do I dim when the sirens blare?
In the spell of that noise too:
our wayward agile selves.

If you blur, my love, it's only because
you are close. But the rhetoric
it creeps like the agile dead, shines
like a searchlight in the second
before the reborn dark. And its figures:
so quick, so unstoppable, so gone.

That day, by the ocean, dipped deep in
the widening dunes and never, for a moment, lost.
If you blur, my love, I suppose it's because
we are close. The prison of the present

unhouses the prison of memory. And suddenly,
I am not at all against memory.
And when they came it was
from the west they came – unhindered, agile,
so good looking and so dead –

in the spell of noise that followed
you lost your vision. But
if you blur, my love –

ON TALKING TO THE ANIMALS

'. . . And seeing, as cosmographers report, that there are nations that have a dog for their king, they must of necessity be able to interpret his voice and motions.'

– Michel de Montaigne,
Apology for Raimond Sebonde

And what if

Orpheus had it easy in his forest
days! – egads Mr S in the croak of sudden
reptillian revelations, earlobes lounging but
alert: hey mister music is but a chink along a blasted plane
of perception ground down ground out with some motor
always on in
the underelectrified morn – alive to hearing, no plane is too high
to hurt the jungle in him, no glass glint or sudden shadow
without fear, he dreams himself a dog and a king of a land
in the woof-confidence of an order far from
the humans in the great poverty of their bloated

frontal lobes, happily neomammalian crunched
in paleomammalian ice, in a cutting plane where the colours fizzle
in globules and the trees grunt alive and doodle
their wishes in the dirt, and the mane is an atmosphere, and art
is useful, for art, mark O Orpheus, is no longer art, labial
as it is in growling unrest, think but a sink into which the inner
and the outer pour, slap the planes
of seeing in purer vision, less exact but also fussier; for when trouble
comes from beyond the savannah and lobe dangles
against lobe, the forest is no more
than the oblong chinks it shows in second slipped
in second plane
of chee-ak, chee-ak, on the muse
of frrrt ffrrrt, on the sssschoo pa-ti-too folds the perfectly
sane drinking
deep the base of the skull, the signal coming to rest, pressed in
reluctant achoo alertness, the way the face turns from
the blast, the way an elephant listens
with feet on the brink, Subby untames himself,
lets the flowers and the lowlier terrestrial stars afloat in
the ruder air drug and dazzle him, smashes
the blameless sun – and when song – which he has invented – no
longer different from that long curving yowl
issued as a record of his glinting neomammalian arc, when song
tapers and stutters in shaking limbs and the crown falls
on the shrivelling head;
and all the species know
their oneness so that

SEPARATION ANXIETY, AKA FRANKENESSENCESTEIN

O how brittle the clouds above how dark the glass
            the sheet that covers me
wired   lit   from under   the light yellow even
in shadow   and in the bathroom
the resident cockroach   scything wings
its brittle antennae   heavy   sagging
            at the tips   ranging   the cloud
that covers us   in sheets   of soot-smoked glass
how dark   how dark this glass   under our lamp
behind the screen   where her missing body glows and
the brittle member of me inside her grows and her eyes
like ecliptic moons   shining behind cloud   and her
                                                                  vein like wire
and my dendrites like wire   rebuilding her   part
by broken part   recently past   a glass
irreplaceable   a cloud   and in the under-lit room
under brittle sheets   under dead sheets
I stitch her hands   those things of beauty   to her wrists

I wire the jaw movable   ventriloquizing
her brittle kisses for her   the glass of
her thighs   her underlit mound   the twin clouds
of her breasts   the crescent   of her bum
and from the smoke   of the gone   her double
wrapped in sheets   rises in the underlit room
                                                  my shadow
under her sheets brittle   as the blue clouds
                                          above

POEM, WITH CHOICES

Drunk on his little bicycle,
not unlike little Nakulan drunk, in his time,
on *his* bicycle, searches Mr S
for drink: in this buttoned-up bloody city, searching
not so much for the sake as for the larger cause
that the tawdry may not have been entirely decimated
by some insecure fellow's prohibitionary zeal, that drink but drink
beyond simulation, that drink may come to redeem
our lives danced around the taxman
and the pulmonary State, drink surviving the machinations of
terminally boring boors, not moral police so much
as goondas raj, goondas fulminating to inherit the goondas
        of yore, oh, no, that we may do
it over, that is overdo it, that we may go drunk
in the very street our souls dragging us by the bit into new lands,
        that lit, like Montaigne,
saying one thing   doing another,
drunk like the fulminating line that does
whatsoever it wants, whosover it wants wher-
ever, flying festooning or drinking
with angry red decimal eyes, dumb

to critics, beyond appraisal, beyond sapience,
clearing the air, fulminating against red
of anger and for the naked hungry greedy monsooned
with the blood of flowers, marooned
on the traffic islands, crooning like elephants to the skies –

*

culminating in the drunk sun of day, rolling awake on the road,
for we shall disavow our decisions, our most daring jumps
    when asked,
for our courage shall fail us later but our work shall remain
    to defend or not itself –

*

culminating not too soon as a kind of nothingbliss
in the drunk degenerate illuminated bed, in the dread fight
against lumbering heavy shadows –

*

culminating where once we began, in that dark basement bar by
    the sea –
the television its single channel, the drunk men solo and silent
working their way down the glasses as if at prayer –

*

garlanded by the light of life itself.

TURBULENCE AT TWENTY THOUSAND FEET

'. . . [W]e know by instinct . . . [how they] cast the shadow of their own destruction.'

The sun has lost its power of speech:
the holy light collected in the palm at dawn:

the barley mill or the water wheel,
which are but fictions to stand

in place of our lives while Commerce tucks
into the cockpit looking unexpectedly avuncular.

And I am scared. I am scared that time wills
to make a bloody mash of me. I am scared

by the lovely palms of my contemporaries,
the bruised palms of their patrons.

Noise is everywhere, truth – who knows. Perhaps noise
is the truth. The cock crows

in the morning of the great epics and
my cock too, in the shallow pit

of my more modest morning. The wind moves the sea
and the palms and, less obviously, the buildings.

Declares himself hereby does Master Subramanearlyunpronoun-
ceableanian
in plain black pant and plain white shirt to the American comrades

with the arrow of history where it meet the still darkening sea
here in the conjoining of our countries the evil they wring together

with hope of some true some different some less cynical alliance
for we manifest that order unknown to us

for look how far we've come in these few years
begging as we do for business as usual

MEMORIES OF FAILED AFFAIRS

From a passing balcony a crow jerked its beard. If crows are indeed the incarnations of our ancestors, then they can be found everywhere, even in the daytime.

At the height of noon when you are tucked away, their shiny coats in the sun, blazing black

like weathercocks on the high, Indo-Saracenic cupolas. And a sari on a clothesline, translucent flute of the wind, now, in the stark heat, dead still.

Passion sleeps curled in the shade. You push your heart forward, inch at a time, not for fear. You pay the rent, the rent pays you.

*

Getting testy, Meester Subra-Teste? Mind a mere cupola disjunct from animating body-proponent?

'Don't misjudge me,' Mr S says. 'If only I could unfurl her sari again, layer by layer like a naughty boy, and she were to speak from her body below, unneeding of Krishna's tele-services, then my body too would make any mind obsolete.'

'Ah,' continues Mr S, 'The body has no proponents but its own degenerate shelf. I shall tug at her sari till her sari comes undone. I shall rent the fineness of that cloth, that silk, that georgette, that gorgeous fineness, she shall thank me for it.'

*

The face falls apart, the cheekbones hollow, crow's feet rasp around the eyes, the forehead betrays a life.

And yet, drawn to the gentle cupolas of her breasts, drawing close, pulling aside, falling near with nose and tongue, in a softness of real passion only passion does cure: I have known this. I have felt it. I cannot say whether it was her or the way her loosened sari fell about me and the light I held her in.

In the middle of that tea field, the way she bent down to take me in her mouth I thought I would love her forever. Nearby, the stream. Around us, the green chequerboard hills. Our love found its purest song in these places, if I may still call it that.

*

Love: a rented word. Crow: a sign, a constant danger.

Is it true the body loves itself only in transcendence?
Is it true teeth are the directest proponents of sexual desire?
Is it true limbs may never be honest if they wish to express
themselves?
Does passion direct or may it be directed?

*

We are sorry to interrupt your lyric for these brief messages. Please stay tuned.

See how the palm waves on the water's edge. That is endurance. It has never been sensual.

On the other hand, stocks and bonds have risen. We like it when they keep going up like that, don't we, up and up forever. Real estate is also mysterious and awesome in this way. Rent is but the mystery encased within. O but to kiss

the memory of her left cupola, the lovely nipple inverted

is not to kiss her breast. Gone are the semantic proponents in your life, Mr S, down to those little heavenly particulates of grammar whose duty is merely to join to join lest evening fall to rent the sentence fall apart in the passional the fineness of sari the eyes in its print show the hard stare of the crow in the shutdown the draining of colour the vivid or the reason to live –

Phew, remarks
Mr S, that
was terribly painful
but somehow
I couldn't bear
to see it end.

The aquanaut emerges to address the press with memory of
things swimming.

The memory of the needle's prick in the old surviving vein.

The blood that fills, lazy in the eye.

DIGRESSION IN RECEIPT OF NOURISHMENT, ACKNOWLEDGEMENT OF THE BODY'S INBUILT GUILT

Dear sir, dear self, in acknowledgement of, in thanks and its other coinside, guilt, for:

humblest receipt of modern life,
neurotic redemption of cultural afterlife,
daily sambar its squelchy redemption
our thought parade – labour, imaginary production,
magic drone drone of the verbal,
magic deceit of referral

deceit of the distant memory of agriculture
and also perhaps in the concrete sense the word production
    that suitor
whose emergence over centuries and subsequent disappearance
made work as evil then work as necessity work as transcendence
in food, food as work, production as receipt of culture, and
    finally magic
because of the lack of effort, the lack of magic.

Hmm, he declares. What a surprise! It is in fact chewable constant food and not culture that is the source of my guilt. That dark and unplaceable drone, which dogs me even in my settled bliss, is nothing less than the mind's receipt of the alimentary canal's relentless production: shit as shamanic.

On hearing this, Mrs S in her teasing voice says: cho tragic. And yet, she says, is this it, are we now in receipt of all the information, are you not merely being a typical old brahmboy, rehearsing and at best recasting food = karma equations? All I really hear in your guilty moan is the ascetic drone of several rather persistent arguments over the centuries of your so-called culture, cultural production advocating, despite its beehive drive, disengagement as a route to freedom!

Nor did the ancients or the moderns crack the guilt of eating in general, concurs he. The answer lies not in the invention of food or the production or the revival of magic. The answer (rubbing mournfully his belly, his liver, his mysterious insides) is here, right here, and it cannot speak, for all its even-now drone.

You are sad when you are hungry, she says, guilty when you are full. Or is it the other way around, lovable drone, hungry *because* sad, full *because* guilty?

Resplendent food of my heart, he says, let me tell you that I am happiest in receipt of your salads. They are of conceptual interest in their sly conundrum of a kitchen's labour,

focusing, as they do, not quite on process but on the deceptive harmony of their elements. They are not guilt-free, but they do address guilt more directly in never fully concealing their sources. How cynically have our salads been engineered into metaphors for political culture; and yet they are the very morsels of culture! Let me celebrate for a second your last effort, that wedding of orange and avocado, let future generations know that bliss exists!

I thank you dear, she says, but salad is not the answer.

Some leave their traces.
Some grasp grace.

SHORT PRAYER TO THE MOON

Moon, though your energies be uncertain, I beseech you, protect him, protect all of us, from our nightly visions.

May the murderer and the hero withdraw gently from this, our despairing prescript.

May daylight return.

May we drink from the cup of gratitude.

May we last long enough to make note of our error.

Though burdened by knowledge, may we walk out into the open.

Though burdened by knowledge, may the clouds lift from our eyes.

Hour by hour, may we learn to free ourselves from prayer.

ON THE NECESSITY OF SPEAKING OF CASTE

First the dreaded fear of caste, wearing its little corset
on trained and bumpy ribs. It stains your vision, corrugates
your fucking body, bawdy as it is and cussed and with
no language to speak of itself
outside of itself. Then a more
untethered fear, of a kind
of polarity, a cathode
leaping current into
the other eyes, a betrayal
a way of merely
repeating with each
denial; you cut away
that plaster cast but your limbs
occupied the same
space they did before. Always
the coast of saying too much versus
the inland of saying little. Often
the boast of castelessness
cast about while coarsening
the mixture in tentative
proffered proof, corset-

ripping, habit cleaning, cross-
questioning each minutae of
self performance for evidential
taint. The problem is
you are no one,

least of all yourself, chatterbox, tubelight,
and any skin scanned curséd acre by curséd acre,
any videograph plotted image by captured
amputated frame, will not unearth the mounting
or final particular, will neither incriminate
nor exonerate. Better head for the coast
of everything, a trip you won't
be coming back from, the death-salve
of total re-polarity; for yank that one thread
of caste and the whole shebang unravels
and no word is sacred: not culture, not history,
not ancestry, not identity, not community(!), not kismet,
    not daddy mummy
thatha paati aham veedu vandi mooku paatu
chappal apple application beating nadai sakkarai confuse
suppose close decide – not even to mention the fruitless farce

of having to footnote the debacle. You can escape to those places
where they've barely heard of it, a little joke, a quaint
curiosity of textbooks, casting yourself
across, casting yourself anew – with your English
in your secret pouch – but that is no escape. There the questions
that dogged your open eyes grow terrifyingly academic where
squared in the brace of not quite similar corollaries your amnesia
buries the whole bone – and the cost no longer shows up
on the balance sheet, even if you're still

paying, back on the coast of caste where
the current is rapidly dragging you into
the deep and everything except the polarities
has shifted, for everything must always shift,
for your senses are no guarantee and
the easiest possible to destabilize
and the handshake of the everyday mocks you
in its forthrightness despite
the downcast eyes, cut across and overwritten and
underwritten by other feints
and fealties going far back or sprouting anew,
submerged deep below the public curse, the demure corset
of citizenship, the bearish casket of implication,
predestination, the cathode's rays reaching to
turn you inside out while the wise
voices say – o silly Mr S give it up, relax, cool it
with that pathetic irritating upper-caste self-flagellation
again, cool it with that uneasiness in yours or
anyone else's skin, cool, the quicksand of your abstractions,
cast yourself into the waves, leave it alive, live
yourself, leave us alone – while the heavens open up
and the cussed gods and the cussed demons and the five
    missing castes
churn the land from the sea, draw in the everlasting distinctions
or at least the idea of distinction and the older boys
gamble over games in the street and the tailor sits in his little room
with the TV on and mends again the corset's seam
and the night broadcasts itself in wave upon wave
up and down and up and down the simmering coast
and what is written comes back to haunt
what has not yet been written

and the dogs howl and bark and howl and the late
workman still hammers at the building and
the stars in truth know nothing of the future
and the foundation is ripped from the torso of the earth.

He brushes a tiny beetle from the chipped corner of the pane. Squinting, he steps back to admire the assonance of his near-identical ears. 'I am the gesture and the body that makes it, I am the gesture and the lungs that breathe.'

HIS OWN OBSOLESCENCE: 4

The Ant

There is the fetish of the new and then
        there is the dream of the new:
if the sun glints through his bedroom pane
        each day glowing without fail
he cannot trust it yet for all that regular
        hokum – needs some kind of shake-up
does he, needs . . . to shuck off his human reservation,
        his dark ant shuffling with rice grain.

Google is a perennial tree that gives no flowers

VIMALA

Undefinable pole. Sharer
of scar: the first

birth water yet unknown
till we met

repeating the planet. Guide friend
in first incarnation

Vimala   nothing given   what
we have between

us is what you a decade ahead
made for us when I

a brand new blinking roughstepping limb
could only barely

perceive, when Michael so cherubic
could sing instinctively

of age. Our scars mysteriously
matching: you arrive at the door

from far: to hold   teach
me in the bath   where

all experience is acquired and the human
now unanimal   grows intimate with

the image: our image Vimala in a second
you change from mother

to brother to father no rules exist
with us   no protocols

to rehearse no ritual marks
the boundaries   where in a corner of the room

a tape recorder plays The Eagles the foreign
refuses to be foreign and the world

shrinks to be. Leading chorister you
chart that outer zone

in those notes you send from afar –
once say when America snowed or

other wonders still wonders then – in
that distance and others

like it is
our closeness born relations

become unbound from birth   the top 40
countdown shows roar

and whistle across the hard estranging
seas, scars pester and muster

their way back into folds
of skin   grow so old

on the very point
of dissolution   and you

the only to whom so much
could be said and heard in the leftover hardness

of what exchanged. And with Lionel
Richie who had been central   quietly

fading from our lives the earth submerging
in the tide   of the years   we are

from instance   to instance   nearly
identical now   and only

closer for the others arrived. Vimala
the spark survives   the earth

survives   John Denver survives
the scars   grow

luminous   you
invented us.

WALKS FOR THE NEAR AND FAR SENSES

The hypertrophied city it is pure food for the shadowy eye, the present ear but the gently discursive nose alas must merely stand its inner hairs on sharpest guard lest the mouth taste more than what is ahem strictly necessary; so the city it spells no more than hollow ecliptic withholding in the elliptical shadows of seemingly purposeless fellows, the men who burrow into eyes searching for something or offering something or the men who just inhere, look straight ahead and don't look at all, puffing on beedis with deeply hollowed cheeks drawing smoke up from the grinding binding remade earth.

This discursive dismissal of the sun in the eclipse of her pout, the way she takes you in snakes that tongue on your shuddering election, prescient willowy wallowing at the base while further dark waves they gather, some great generator rumbles awake, turbines howl discursively, present lips to a shadowy mouth of the newish city some rebellious sonny has fanned for his pleasure – even if elsewhere his father's father, firm and unsmiling, ensconced in a frame, a hand-embroidered image, appears to be looking calmly away, casting no shadow on his son, our son's father, sitting below, much looking the same, wearing the same topi, sitting at his true teak desk, what else, dismissing flies with light flicks of fingers.

The slip of the present, diesel's dastardly incense – the mall – imitates and magnifies the old world bungalow, luring then clouting visitors in wave upon wave upon entry, but the road to the mall must come from what used to be called the pagoda which is much older and elliptical as tend to be the paths of the previous and moreover, on the way to the great cowshed-like structure over the great cowbell-like mound that the city's garbage feeds into day by callow day snakes also the colonial canal that once fed us and now engorged turbid can only eat us in all the exhausted fume of a body that, seated in an East–West axis, takes a quick tremor like the briefest of shallow glances, not shaking but rapidly vibrating, amidst coolness and relaxed impotency; which means that on occasions when the current's greater grid quakes sympathetically and the electricity snaps, the whole continuity suddenly shows itself to have lasted the length of a shadow, a willowy divagation of thought, plunging us out of ourselves and into the curious re-animation of those lanes.

Then questions to himself Mr S, might one detect one's own odour, can one in fact sniff deep into one's armpits in order to objectively know what it is what one has truly absorbed of what of the enveloping incense of this optimistically dubbed metropolis in fairly immeasurable scale and detail is instantiatingly given, what a part of, what may not be divided, what not thrown away nor dismissed, what exuded, what exhausted, what claimed, what shared, what spilled, what lost, what known, what worthy of investigation, what taken up on consultation, what exorbitantly touted, what carried in single file, what covered with bright yellow bathroom tiles, what burrowed with moistened workmen, what daintily hidden behind a cloth screen in a cycle rickshaw, what coughed from the crudest of conical speakers, what smoke suspended like sculpture, what mangling flyoverist vista, what eclipse arrived in our tunnels, what hollow in place of the eyes, what harvest of mud, what hand-written letter, what tuneless call, what sudden field, what ball bouncing dark?

FATHER OF MR S

My dear Appa, would you mind very much
if I borrowed your memory? I feel such an odd deficit
in not having heard Madurai Mani
at three in the morning
in some darkened Tanjore
river town. The years
are a lousy
microphone and damaged
in recording what is left
of his singing can now
only but trace
a raucous crackle
in my head. Ah but I speak
your English, wear your pants; why
o why must I feel useless
amidst your life's unlikely reach?

Appakins, fronds of banana
leaves hang uncut in
the knot of a grove. My memory
is armour: sometimes it even half-shuts
me out. You are teaching yourself
Swahili, you are teaching yourself
French. You are Chinese. You are holding
a video cassette like an idol
to the light of worship. Your mouth
is open, your eyes asquint, your
head cocked. You are singing
without a trace of sound. I am clinging
to your sleeve.

Appa, I still wonder about My Tamil:
shall it be Your
Tamil (you know
what I mean) or must I strive
even harder towards
a recombinant street? Will
it be your Kaveri
or an Indian
Ocean that yet
might be mine? What
about Musiri who grabs
me by the hearticles
but whom you
even in those days
never could quite
bring yourself
to like? Shall I tuck
my shirt in
or hang it all out? And am
I, should I
not be
as much my Amma
as my Appa? Ah
for mere years
ago the answers
to all of these so
instant. Now some
more ancient reflex
triggers proclivities caught

at a helpless reactive
age. I mix a right
and wrong me, mumble
doubled up
talk.

Appa, my friend, my
dear rascal, it is thanks to you
I never feared
water. Perhaps
as a child I quietly
studied your grace
in chores, your meditative
ironing of
the clothes hovering
between method and
unrazed space. Yet
to my untrained eyes it
was odd: you were
odd. In the years when
you sang most freely I
could not digest you and
now, when I can follow closely
that GNB-style bruga or that high
piercing voice, you
are not able to sing
as you did before. Still
let them be, these few
convergent years.

My dear Appa sir, permit me
to catch your collar for
a moment and ask: when
will you ever get round
to writing that requested
memoir? Promise it will
be honest and naughty, as
you are, now,
among us. Let the hazy moonlit
past consist of more than a succession
of bland unimpeachable
deities. Let not all
the men be noble, nor all the deeds
good. Let history do more
than wag that strict Sanskritic
finger, let it carry instead the black
silt of the stream
where once you kicked
and cried.

Ah for how long should he struggle with the uninvited one.
For the uninvited one he names himself.

HIS OWN OBSOLESCENCE: 5

The Ruse of the Blank Slate

There's something even stranger going
on here. Mr S longed
for the idea of progress because he couldn't
stand what he was, never mind the hokum of
progress. In 1951, for instance, in S's
father's era, the manager of the New Project to Shake
Things Up and Rain Marvels of Engineering on
the Landscape to Herald the New India was looking
specifically for young Brahmin boys from the South not
unlike himself in his youth to hire for his scheme
up North in Orissa, and the little marvels they arrived
and presented themselves by the trainload
far from anything they thought of as home; and in
the hostels they replicated food
and habits, opened and closed

to the world around. So did paradoxically the old
persist among the glinting new; people stuffed
their faces to live on as they had and
had not before. He'd kill

for a blank slate, caress that lovely fetish.
But the body is not a blank slate.

IN-LAW OF S

My brother: brother though brother made by human design
    and no
especially deserving biology; choice indeed though

certainly not my own; jig-dancing alien buffoon
manifesting one day in our living room

so bizarre and yet – how could it be? – so right –
accidentally you completed us better than fate

or custom, simple will or jiggered scripture (preservative
measures which somehow in the very stale and rebarbative

crust they harden turn equally unaccountable loss).
My brother: the other hand: my pig- and cow-eating
    Walloon, my piss-

taking, law-book thumping, stock price memorizing, labour
un-alienating, seat-reserving, liquor-loving wunder-

bah: your alien speech, your hidden power reserves, your own
unuttered but unwavering rules, applied diligent in the midst
    of prone

and relentless chicanery – and our jagged nervous mugs,
    our shudder
upon the non-returnable admittance of a variety of other

species into this system so carefully conserved by habit and by
    caution and
perhaps almost pathological laws of modesty; then, our new man

made rewiring of pre-rigged laws, a fresh and altogether
different idea of sacred: a breath by which to power

the zeppelin into treacherous futuristic skies thanks
in no small part to you. My brother, the thought sinks

in, Did we deserve you, you us? Evolution (aka the universe)
happily thankfully refrains from commentary on its many bursts

of improbable planning. The human in jigs and apparently
    foolish jags
reassembles; alien gets necessary, banal – affection, like an old dog's
    tail, wags on.

Ah, sleep. How hard it is for some.

MR S'S DATA

Surprisingly he did not read the paper today.

He reads it normally without fail.

There were portable databases there that you could eat after you were done with them, going for practically free.

The newspaper's terrors are surely worse than ours.

The day is really drifting now.

I wonder if I could even have used that database, thinks he. 'Well, I could have *been* that database,' says his laptop to him, unusually eloquent. 'Just that it's hard to *be*.'

Only in mind's stillness shall the wood-apple appear.

HIS OWN OBSOLESCENCE: 6

Getting Back to Basics

lunchtime, so what's new again is rawest hunger
which you can really only fetishize for so long

the mind might glint but the limbs they groan
worthless becomes the hokum of the spoken

O what if art could shake you then
feed you till you were happy and spent

HE ADMITS HE IS DELIRIOUS IN THINKING OF HOW HE CARRIED HER*

'I am delirious in thinking of how I carried you,
I know it in your mime of my delirium to me.
And at dawn when our attention turns to

each other, we smother our every
revenge, we garble thought, mangle
words, recall in kisses how we

carried us. From the tango tangle
of that stone's revenge, our mime of pain
in release of attention in release from the angle

of that construction, I, insane
to the smell of you, the irrelevant
weight of you, the invisible rain

---

*Yes, for then in the midst of our Subbu's guttered attention, she arrives. / Our fellow hardly knows – so long has he held implicit conviction in the mimetic function of art to be wed to suffering, as painted horns to bullock-cart, as in the centuries of dreary weddings before him, to be bred implacably / in unhappiness. // Might one then continue, if one no longer harboured revenge? Might anger go the way of revenge? Might resentment pucker up, flicker off?

on the dawn of you, the errant
world in that klepto-nanosecond, that shrine
immaterial, that materialized present –

for our attentions are sometimes too available,
for restlessness of the forklifts threatens
the very truth of dawn, renders it metaphorical,

for in that moment I carried you down
from that ledge and you felt
impossibly light we were graceful,

that you in fact must have carried me carrying you
in order for it to have been possible, the idea
that for the exact length of a suspended thought

mimesis and truth were one, dawning
and attention equal, anger set aside, space
opened its vacuum to clarity so clarity – like
the unspoken composite beloved – could appear.'

who could have thought your curdled-milk smell

'THAT TOUCH OTHERWORLDLY . . .'

That touch otherworldly   that foot from within her
beyond   and when he felt
that foot he saw that fire at play
a long red lash curving down the sky   leaping
from roof to ravenous roof needing all and
everywhere heat like screen pressed to
nose for in the touch all instances returned
and all was touch and every tiny
hurt once rained stung back
unforgotten raw of a shin scraped   bee
still swollen below his eye   and then
those hot gravel stones he'd stepped on
spoke with their rattle and the tin
of the roofs he'd felt as if it were his own
wilted in the heat and all of life
as scarce as an afternoon crouched
on the bus he never got off   plunging into
the road as if in descent the seat leaned
back and the view's spinning concussive
jumps   this play like hands on
his window   which was the play

of heat on his face or indeed his father's
face as a child in the moment of song
grown legible   my hand pressed on
a shoulder and the killing air
of the evening in the evening's sweetest
spot when all smells are wet against
the weight of the day
behind   the people in long hours
at work   quarrying stone   the bluest
plastic bag its fin caught
in the breeze in the face
in a tangle of arms in
noise   a beating on the skin
or deep in one long
hour he a stranger clapped
his hand on your thigh and
you knew the need
and the disgust of it   the warmth
and the terror tingle   the pure
anger of it   hairs
speaking to hairs and the train
in long profile and the passengers
bodiless   then among
those conjured hurt and browning
leaves that fine dust of future   this
this first foot's print against the wall
of her medium   this heart beating from
outside in   and he in his helpless
worship of her   in these
visions folded in flashes   sloppily
circumscribed   and then from

nowhere claps father time which
was me and I spring from your hands
and I spring from your face as
you now someone else   spring
from my groin   my
continuous skin   yoked   but
nowhere   did my hands flutter
although that had become
their nature   nowhere could
I lose my grip   in that ever
growl all of me was   and I swam
swam in every direction burned
in pinpricks
wrung hollow by the night
and I was one among the ants
signalling to them
and even the light green of
my shirt hurt me   and all colour
was too much when
the play of the world
magnified to surround
this seed   its faint brush
its foot   its unknowing face
its cortex   its spine
its first taste   my touch
otherworldly.

NOTES

p. 8 – '*Thiruvalluvar*': A celebrated Tamil poet dated to between second century BC and eighth century AD who lived, according to legend, in Mylapore, an area now part of the city of Chennai, notional location of most of the Mr S poems. The particular reference here is to a temple dedicated to Thiruvalluvar in present-day Mylapore, where one can find him as a plaster idol.

p. 10 – '*Parthasarathy's Cilappatikaram*': The Cilappatikaram is a key epic of ancient Tamil literature, dated to somewhere around the beginning of the common era. Kannagi is its female protagonist.

In the epic's central episode, Kannagi and her husband Kovalan arrive as strangers to the walled city of Madurai. Kovalan goes into the city to pawn Kannagi's anklet, is wrongfully framed for the theft of the queen's own anklet, and is summarily executed. Possessed by a semi-divine fury, Kannagi avenges his death by tearing off her left breast and throwing it at the city, which then catches fire and is burned down.

My poem makes particular reference to a translation of the epic by R. Parthasarathy (Columbia University Press, 1992 / Penguin India, 2004), and also to the use of mnemonics (*vaaypaatu*) – 'sweet mango', etc. – to figure ancient Tamil prosodic feet. See Parthasarathy's afterword to the book, p. 359 of the Penguin edition.

p. 28 – '*Thyagaraja*' (1767–1847): A key composer of South Indian art music, who might be described as neo-Romantic and who, at least according to legend, deliberately refused royal patronage.

p. 50 – '*Nakulan*': An important Modernist poet and prose writer in Tamil, influenced by Joyce and Simone Weil, who enjoyed getting completely drunk and then riding around his home city of Trivandrum on a bicycle.

p. 52 – '*. . . [W]e know by instinct . . .*': The quote is taken from W.G. Sebald's novel *Austerlitz*.

'Why language? They
ask, why not medicine
or magic? Why not
something more useful?'
(Kala Krishnan Ramesh)

The editors at HarperCollins believe that poetry is medicine, magic and more. Committed to publishing the most exciting contemporary poetry from India and the subcontinent, we wanted to celebrate ten of our favourite books by publishing them as special keepsake editions under the 'Poetry 10' series. From sci-fi verse to modern bhakti poetry, long narrative sequences about birth and identity to brief sonnets, each book will speak to lovers (and haters) of poetry with wit, wisdom, clarity and abandon.

3 Sections by Vijay Seshadri
All One's Blue by Kazim Ali
Bearings by Karthika Naïr
Countries of the Body by Tishani Doshi
He Is Honey, Salt and the Most Perfect Grammar by Kala Krishnan Ramesh
Life & Times of Mr S by Vivek Narayanan
Malabar Mind by Anita Nair
Space Gulliver: Chronicles of an Alien by Sampurna Chattarji
Triage: Casualties of Love and Sex by Margaret Mascarenhas
When God Is a Traveller by Arundhathi Subramaniam

Vivek Narayanan's *Life and Times of Mr S* is a book-length sequence of poems exploring identity and what may or may not constitute it: family, speech patterns, a homeland or two, caste, literary heritage, class, gender, desire, food. Woven around the person of Mr S, the poems morph into dazzling narrative forms that expand and challenge all traditional definitions of a living language. Richly textured and eccentric, parodic and poignant, this is a book of poems that should be read and then reread.